THE ANCIENT WORLD

ANCIENT ROME

BY PETER BENOIT

CHILDREN'S PRESS®
AN IMPRINT OF SCHOLASTIC INC.
NEW YORK TORONTO LONDON AUCKLAND SYDNEY
MEXICO CITY NEW DELHI HONG KONG
DANBURY, CONNECTICUT

Content Consultant
Josiah Osgood, PhD
Professor of Classics
Georgetown University
Washington, D.C.

Library of Congress Cataloging-in-Publication Data
Benoit, Peter, 1955–
  Ancient Rome/by Peter Benoit.
      p. cm.—(The ancient world)
  Includes bibliographical references and index.
  ISBN-13: 978-0-531-25183-6 (lib. bdg.) — ISBN-13: 978-0-531-25983-2 (pbk.)
  1. Rome—History—Juvenile literature. 2. Rome—Civilization—Juvenile literature. I. Title.
  DG77.B443 2012
  937—dc23   2012000502

Photographs © 2013: Alamy Images: 31 (Chris Hellier), 11, 16 (Classic Image), 39 (Dattatreya), 58 (FLPA), 21, 28, 82, 87, 92,
100 (INTERFOTO), 18 (Ivy Close Images), 12 bottom (Jeff Greenberg), 66, 80, 95 top, 102 top (Lebrecht Music and Arts Photo
Library), 55 (Lordprice Collection), 19 (Marshall Ikonography), 37, 84 top (Peter Horree), 9 (Photo Art Collection (PAC)), 38, 90
(The Art Gallery Collection), 62 (TPM Photostock), 65 (Walter Bibikow/Jon Arnold Images Ltd.), 96 (William Ju); AP Images:
45 bottom (John Duricka), 15, 29, 40, 103 bottom (North Wind Picture Archives); Bridgeman Art Library: 10 (Giovanni Battista
(1696-1770)/Villa Valmarana ai Nani, Vicenza, Italy/© Luca Sassi), 42 (Louvre, Paris, France/Alinari), 68 (Museo della Civilta
Romana, Rome, Italy/Giraudon), 34 (Peter Jackson (1922-2003)/Private Collection/© Look and Learn), 30, 33, 101 top, 102 bottom
(Tancredi Scarpelli (1866-1937)/Private Collection/© Look and Learn); Corbis Images/Charles & Josette Lenars: 85; Dreamstime:
cover left inset, back cover top, 3 (Dimedrol68), 60 top (Feltmountain), cover main (Jovannig), 6 (Luciano Mortula), 61 (Maria
Feklistova), 64 (Raluca Tudor); Getty Images: 56 (After C.C Perkins/The Bridgeman Art Library), 93 (Hulton Archive), 14
(Sebastiano Ricci/The Bridgeman Art Library); iStockphoto: 7 (Moodboard_Images), page borders throughout (Julie Macpherson);
Media Bakery/Monashee Frantz: 95 bottom; National Geographic Stock/H.M. Herget: 32; Photo Researchers: 71 top (Marcello
Bertinetti), 81 (Patrick Landmann); Shutterstock, Inc.: 35 (A E O), 8 (Frank Bach), 84 bottom (fstockfoto), 88 (grafalex), 4, 41
(Jens Stolt), 91 (kelis), 13 (Khirman Vladimir), 71 bottom (Natursports), 59 (Paolo Gianti), 44 (Rostislav Glinsky); Superstock,
Inc.: 5, 12 top, 53, 70, 73, 74, 83 (DeAgostini), 57 (Fine Art Images), cover right inset, 1 (Image Asset Management Ltd.), 48
(imagebroker.net), 86 (Melvin Longhurst), 60 bottom (Science Faction), 72 (Universal Images Group), 36, 98 (Visual & Written),
45 top; The Granger Collection: 94, 103 top (F. Schoenberg), 23, 24, 27, 43, 46, 47, 89; The Image Works: 76 (BeBa/Iberfoto), 78,
79 (J Williamson/Lebrecht), 20, 50, 77 (Mary Evans Picture Library), 25, 51, 52, 69, 101 bottom (North Wind Picture Archives).

Maps by XNR Productions, Inc.

All rights reserved. Published in 2013 by Children's Press, an imprint of Scholastic Inc.
Printed in the United States of America 113

1 2 3 4 5 6 7 8 9 10 R 22 21 20 19 18 17 16 15 14 13

The ancient Romans constructed buildings from concrete very similar to that used in building projects today.

JOURNEY BACK TO ANCIENT ROME

Many modern buildings are based on ancient Roman architecture.

More than half the words in the English language come from ancient Rome.

TABLE OF CONTENTS

Roman coins

The Past Is Present

See for yourself how ancient Rome is still present in our lives today.

A statue of a Lar,
a god of the home

THE BIRTHPLACE OF WESTERN CIVILIZATION

The modern world rests on a foundation established long ago in Rome. Many of the most basic aspects of our daily lives have roots in Roman ingenuity and innovation. More

Many ancient Roman ruins still stand today.

than half of the words in the English language have their origins in Rome, and the alphabet we use to write them was spread throughout Europe by the Roman Empire. Much of our legal system, from the wording of laws to the most basic features of our courts, owes a debt to ancient Rome.

Rome was also a technologically advanced society. Its superior military engineering largely drove its military success and conquests. A Roman legion, an army unit of about five thousand men,

Many modern legal systems are based on ideas that began in ancient Rome.

could swiftly build roads, base camps, and bridges in a matter of days. In peacetime, they regularly turned these same skills to civilian projects.

Rome's invention of concrete in the third century BCE spurred extensive road building and a host of architectural innovations. Domes, arches, and vaults appeared in theaters, bridges, and temples. The dome of the Pantheon, built about 126 CE, has a diameter of 142 feet (43 meters). It remained the world's largest dome until the construction of the

The interior of the dome of the Pantheon is famous for its geometric design.

dome in the Santa Maria del Fiore cathedral in Florence, Italy, more than thirteen hundred years later.

Rome's engineering technology made entertainment possible on a grand scale. Rome's Colosseum, built in the first century CE, was more than just an architectural marvel. Capable of holding almost fifty thousand spectators, it also was the scene of public executions, battle reenactments, and gladiatorial contests. Spectators roared their approval as strong men fought against wild animals or against one another, with death the likely outcome.

But even the Colosseum paled in comparison with Rome's Circus Maximus. An oval nearly 400 feet (122 m) wide and more than 2,000 feet (610 m) long, it was used for dangerous chariot races that were the talk of the town.

Equally as grand as its entertainment, fascinating as its architectural innovations, and enduring as its laws and language are Rome's mythology and history. The two can scarcely be separated. From the mythological founding of Rome by Romulus and Remus to the madness of Caligula, who reputedly wished to appoint his horse to political office, ancient Rome was a place and time like no other. Amazing in its own right, it is woven through the fabric of our own place and time.

Thousands of people filled the seats of the Circus Maximus during chariot races.

CHAPTER ONE

BORN FROM MYTH

Rome's earliest days are cloaked in myth. Romans always used two stories to explain the origins of their city. In one, the Trojan hero Aeneas wandered westward after the fall of Troy,

According to legend, Aeneas was the son of the goddess Aphrodite.

landing in Italy, where he waged war against a local king, Turnus. Victorious, Aeneas established the port city Lavinium, 19 miles (31 kilometers) south of what would become Rome. The myth linked Rome to the rulers of Troy, giving it a distinctive heritage in the Greek-dominated Mediterranean basin. When the Roman poet Virgil wrote of the Trojan War in the first century BCE, his Aeneas, both **pious** and courageous in battle, became an example of the ideal Roman.

Another origin myth, almost as old as that of Aeneas, was perhaps more important. According to this story, Numitor, the king of an ancient city in what is now Italy, was defeated in battle by his younger brother, Amulius. When Numitor's daughter, Rhea Silvia, gave birth to twins fathered by the warrior-god Mars, Amulius feared their vengeance and ordered them cast into the flooding Tiber River. The basket in which they floated washed ashore close to a sacred fig tree, Ficus Ruminalis, near the Palatine Hill. There, the twins were nurtured by a she-wolf, a creature sacred to Mars, until the royal herdsman Faustulus rescued them. The herdsman and his wife, Acca Larentia, raised the twins Romulus and Remus to be mighty warriors.

Virgil's epic poem The Aeneid *tells the story of Aeneas over the course of 12 books.*

pious (PYE-uhs) practicing a religion faithfully and seriously

The Past Is Present
KEEPING COUNT

Servius Tullius's introduction of the **census** program in the sixth century BCE helped shape the way Rome was governed in the following centuries. The word *census* comes from the Latin word for "estimate," as the census provided Roman leaders with an estimate of the city-state's population and of how many people fell into each wealth class. The Roman census was held every five years, and failure to register for the census was punishable by death.

Today, the influence of the Roman census has spread to many governments around the world. In addition to providing an estimated population count, modern censuses often measure other

important information about the gender, age, ethnicity, and marital status of a nation's people. Governments use this information to plan for growth in certain areas, assign elected officials to different regions, and other important administrative tasks.

A statue of Romulus and Remus drinking milk from a wolf stands today in the modern city of Rome, Italy.

The twins removed Amulius from power and restored Numitor as king. They established a walled settlement atop the Palatine Hill. The new settlement, Rome, was named for Romulus, who became its first king after killing Remus.

The story of Romulus and Remus explains the origin of Roman institutions and kingship. It also places the earliest appearance of Rome atop the Palatine Hill. Archaeologists have found evidence of several small, isolated hilltop settlements on the Palatine and other peaks, some dating before 1,000 BCE. The Palatine village, the earliest, is a small cluster of circular and oval dwellings surrounded by a wood-reinforced clay wall. Such settlements were the seeds that grew into ancient Rome.

census (SEN-suhs) an official count of all the people living in a country or district

Tarquin the Elder (right) established both the Cloaca Maxima and the Circus Maximus during his reign.

By the eighth and seventh centuries BCE, Rome had grown in size and sophistication. Its inhabitants had cleared the wooded hillsides and drained swamps in low valleys to take advantage of rich agricultural land. They freely traded handicrafts with one another and with the Greeks. Those who became wealthy through trade formed an **aristocratic** class. By the seventh century BCE, Rome's fifth king, Tarquin the Elder, built a massive sewer system, the Cloaca Maxima. The sewer was essential to the further development of Rome. It drained the swamp that dominated the valley between the Capitoline, Aventine, and Palatine Hills, and removed wastes from the rapidly growing city-state.

The project also encouraged the gradual development of the Roman Forum, which became the center of Roman life. The Forum was Rome's principal public square. Triumphal processions of victorious military leaders were held there, as well as battles between gladiators and wild animals. The Forum was also, for a time, the commercial center of the city. Over time, balconies

aristocratic (uh-riss-tuh-KRAT-ik) belonging to the upper social classes

The Roman Forum was a bustling center of activity.

The scholar Varro wrote more than six hundred books, covering a wide variety of topics.

were built above shops to provide a better vantage point for viewing the spectacle of lavish gladiatorial contests. Elections were held in the Forum, and orators spoke eloquently before assembled citizens. Criminal trials were commonly held there. The Forum was also home to a vast array of temples, arches, and smaller monuments. Many of them, though now in ruins, still stand today.

THE LEGENDARY KINGS

According to Roman scholar Varro in the first century BCE, Rome was ruled by seven kings from its founding in 753 BCE until an uprising ousted its last king, Tarquin the Proud, in 509 BCE. There is reason to question Varro's history, which is probably a mix of fact and legend. It seems unlikely that the kings reigned for an average of thirty-five years each at a time when life expectancy was much less than that. In addition, many of the era's records were lost when the Senones, a tribe from Gaul, attacked Rome in 386 BCE. As a result, modern historians generally accept that the six monarchs Varro mentions after Romulus were genuine historical figures, but agree that either the era of kingship was significantly shorter or there were more kings, their names now lost.

It seems certain that kingship was not passed down from father to son, but was rather an elected position. The king's power was absolute. He was at once Rome's **ambassador** in negotiating with foreign powers and its chief executive. As the city-state's chief **legislator**, the king created laws that were passed by the Curiate Assembly. Only the king or his appointed *tribunus celerum*, the leader of the king's bodyguards, could call together the Assembly. The king also issued **decrees** with the force of law. All affairs of state, with the notable exception of declarations of war against foreign nations, could be enacted by decree. War could be declared only with the approval of the Assembly and the Senate, which acted mainly as an advisory council. The king was commander in chief of Rome's army. He alone could appoint leaders of divisions of infantry and cavalry.

The king served as judge in all cases of law, both civil and criminal. He was also head priest of Rome. As head priest, he was responsible for communicating messages between the state and the gods. In the earliest times, the king was also in charge of augury, which was a way of determining the will of the gods by examining the flight of birds. Observing and interpreting such signs was considered more important than any public business, including the founding of Rome itself. He appointed religious officers, including members of Rome's four colleges of priests. The king wore a white silk crown and red shoes. He usually wore a distinctive **toga** of white wool decorated with a purple border.

Rome's second king, Numa Pompilius, is described as a peacemaker in most writings. After the death of Romulus, factions within Rome fought for control. The Senate ruled Rome for a year until Romulus's successor could be chosen. Numa finally became

ambassador (am-BAS-uh-dor) official sent by a government to represent it in another country

legislator (LEJ-is-lay-tur) official with the power to make or change laws

decrees (di-KREEZ) official decisions or orders

toga (TOH-guh) a piece of clothing worn by people in ancient Rome; it was wrapped around the body and draped over the left shoulder

Roman kings relied on augury to help them make important decisions.

annexing (AN-eks-ing) taking control of a country or territory by force

king in 715 BCE. Pious and claiming to be inspired by the gods, he eased tensions between rival factions.

Tullus Hostilius succeeded Numa in 672 BCE. Unlike Numa, he was constantly at war and cared little for religious observances. He is credited with defeating and **annexing** Alba Longa, an ancient city southeast of Rome. Tullus also built the Curia Hostilia, the first Senate, on rising ground at the northwest boundary of the Forum. Through all of its later changes, it remained the center of political life in Rome for hundreds of years.

Ancus Marcius, Numa's grandson, succeeded Tullus in 642 BCE. Ancus promptly restored the gods to importance in Roman life. He also defeated and annexed several neighboring villages, making their inhabitants Roman citizens. Ancus expanded Rome's boundaries and influence to the Tyrrhenian Sea, where he established Ostia, a major port city.

Ostia eventually became crucial for supplying the city of Rome with imported food.

According to one legend, Servius Tullius's head once mysteriously burst into flames when he was a child.

His successor, Tarquin the Elder (in 616 BCE), established the Circus Maximus, annexed several more cities, and built a stone wall around the city. Rome grew quickly in population, prestige, and wealth during his reign. When Tarquin was assassinated in 578 BCE, Servius Tullius was elevated to kingship. Servius was popular with Rome's lower-class citizens, whose position in life he consistently worked to improve. He developed the first census for Rome's population and established voting rights based on a firm foundation of five economic classes that were organized according to wealth. Servius also established the Century Assembly, which replaced the Curiate Assembly.

To accommodate Rome's territorial acquisitions and newer settlements, Servius expanded the original boundaries of Rome that had been established by Romulus. He built a mighty stone wall around the new boundaries of the city and divided the people of Rome into four tribes. He also reformed the army and made lasting contributions to religion.

The assassination of Servius Tullius allowed Tarquin the Proud to take control of Rome.

hereditary (huh-RED-i-ter-ee) passed from parent to child

consuls (KAHN-suhlz) high-ranking officials of the Roman government

republic (ri-PUHB-lik) a form of government in which the people have the power to elect representatives who manage the government

patrician (puh-TRIH-shun) a member of one of the noble families of ancient Rome

plebeians (pli-BEE-uhnz) the common people of ancient Rome

In 535 BCE, Servius was overthrown by Tarquin the Proud and assassinated in the streets of Rome. Several senators loyal to the fallen king were also murdered. Tarquin was married to Servius's daughter, Tullia, who aided her husband in her father's demise. According to legend, she ran over her father's corpse with her chariot and returned home drenched in his blood. Tarquin soon plunged Rome into war. When he suggested making Rome's kingship **hereditary**, he was overthrown and forced out of Rome. A new government led by a pair of **consuls**, annually elected by citizens, replaced the monarchy. Rome was set on a new course.

REPUBLIC

Rome's transition from kingship to **republic** in 509 BCE caused widespread social, economic, and political changes. During the first years of the republic, political power lay firmly in the hands of the **patrician** class. A citizen could be a patrician only by birth, and both parents had to be patricians. Patricians could not legally marry **plebeians**. Plebeians were excluded from the Senate, religious leadership, and most other positions of power.

The patrician class kept the laws secret. Plebeians were forbidden to know the laws but could be punished severely for breaking them. In 494 BCE, plebeians—unable to make the patrician elite listen to their grievances concerning food shortages, debt relief, and unequal land distribution—abandoned Rome together. They formed their own assembly and elected officers from among their number. The state was threatened by an enemy attack, but the plebeians refused military service. Rome's leaders were forced to make concessions so the plebeians would return and help them fight. Patrician leaders granted the Plebeian Council a limited right to pass resolutions pertaining to all the people of Rome.

Rome had little choice in dealing with the social unrest of its poorer citizens. The plebeians, who greatly outnumbered the patricians, were central to the state's economic and military life. It would have been disastrous to disregard them in the midst of the

Plebeians were considered low-class citizens in ancient Rome.

early republic's military campaigns. Rome achieved **hegemony** on the Italian Peninsula in the first half of the third century BCE by conquest and consolidation. One group after another joined the Roman alliance. A state continuously at war could scarcely afford unrest at home or within the ranks of its military machine.

In control of the peninsula, Rome next confronted Carthage for control of Sicily, annexing it at the successful conclusion of the First

Punic War (264–241 BCE). Rome then gained Sardinia in 238 BCE. Twenty years later, Rome gained more Carthaginian provinces in Spain after the Carthaginian general Hannibal's invasion of Italy was repelled. Rome followed with conquests of Macedonia and Greece, and also annexed territories in Asia Minor and Asia.

During the First Punic War, the Roman navy defeated the Carthagnians at the Battle of Mylae.

Thanks to these conquests, Rome's elite became fabulously wealthy. The conquest of Greece brought elements of Greek culture into the mainstream of Roman intellectual life. At the same time, greater wealth encouraged upper-class Romans to occupy very large pieces of land in southern Italy. These acquisitions openly defied a 367 BCE law setting the maximum land holding of any person at 330 acres (134 hectares). War captives were enslaved to work on these **latifundia**, which soon displaced small, less productive farms. Because only landowners could serve in the military, Rome's military began to shrink as latifundia became common and peasant landowners were forced to give up their property. Countless men were set adrift. The times were ripe for revolution.

When the government official Tiberius Gracchus pushed for enforcement of the 330-acre (134 ha) limit on landholdings in 133 BCE, several senators had him murdered. Twelve years later, his brother Gaius met a similar end when he suggested sweeping reforms for more even distribution of wealth and land. Its army weakened, Rome was unable to deal with a Sicilian slave revolt and Italy's invasion by Germanic tribes. Only the fateful decision to arm the landless staved off military disaster. However, the arrangement deepened the frustration of Rome's underclass and encouraged civil war.

Military crises abroad provided popular generals such as Pompey and Crassus with opportunities at home. Pompey was frustrated when Rome's leadership blocked his efforts to get land allotments for his returning army, so he formed a pact in 60 BCE with Crassus and Julius Caesar. The three soon became a strong presence in the Roman government. After Crassus was killed at

The Roman navy was successful at defeating the Carthaginian fleet in a First Punic War battle at Cape Ecnomus.

Tiberius Gracchus was murdered for attempting to make laws of land ownership fairer for the people of Rome.

the Battle of Carrhae in 53 BCE, conflict began to develop between Pompey and Caesar. Pompey feared that Caesar would overthrow him upon returning from his military campaign in Gaul. Caesar was ordered to lay down his arms. Instead, he and his men crossed the Rubicon, a small river in northern Italy, to confront Pompey, who fled south. Pompey was eventually defeated, and Caesar declared himself dictator-for-life of Rome.

Caesar immediately set about a full-scale reform of Roman government, threatening the Roman Republic. In response, a group of more than sixty senators plotted Caesar's assassination. On March 15, 44 BCE, at a meeting of the Senate being held at the Theater of Pompey, the gang of "liberators" killed Caesar by stabbing him twenty-three times. Rome erupted in civil war. The republic, in its final days, would not be restored.

Julius Caesar and his men crossed the Rubicon to lead an attack against the forces of Pompey.

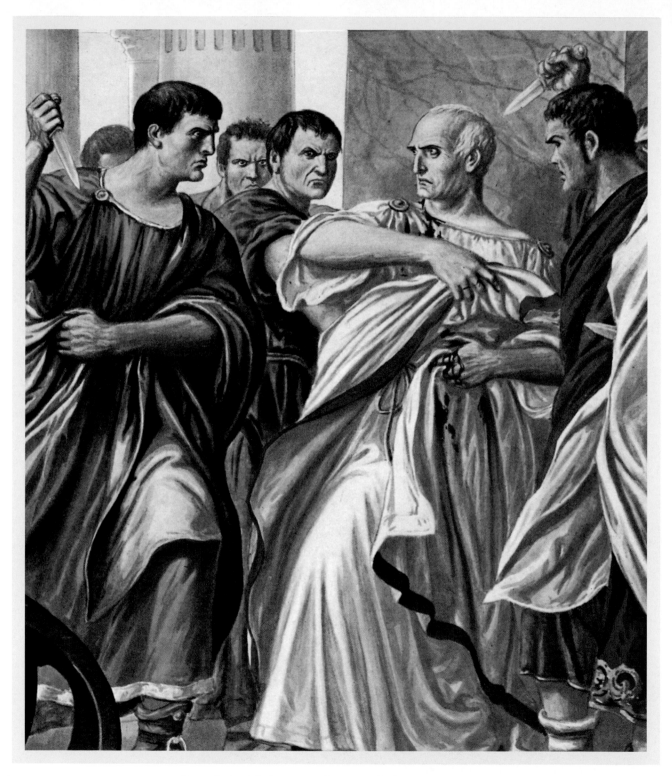

Caesar's death led to major changes in the Roman government.

EMPIRE

Historians date the beginning of the Roman Empire to 27 BCE, when the Senate awarded Octavian, a relative of Caesar, with the title Augustus (meaning "revered one"). This effectively made him Rome's first emperor. In the early years of the empire, overseas colonization helped to ease class tensions over land distribution.

Augustus served as the emperor of Rome until his death in 14 CE.

Augustus was the first in a long succession of Roman emperors. As time went on, severe tensions arose between these emperors and Rome's political elite. Such tensions frequently erupted in violence. Executions and trials for treason were common. The absence of an established law of succession created distrust, intrigue, and power plays within the imperial family. The situation was made worse by the declaration that the emperor was merely first among equals—a nod to the values of the republic—when he in fact wielded far greater power.

The emperors' personalities and behaviors often inspired intense hatred from other government officials. The third emperor,

Emperor Gaius Caesar earned the childhood nickname Caligula, meaning "Little Boot."

Legend holds that Emperor Nero set Rome ablaze and watched it burn.

Caligula, required senators to kiss his feet, and many sources claim that he was insane. Nero—who, at age sixteen, commanded an empire of 2 million square miles (5 million sq km) and 55 million people—chose to indulge his love of chariot racing instead of paying attention to Rome's large standing army and threats to the eastern territories. In 59 CE, he ordered his own mother executed for aiding in a plot to have him replaced by a political rival. When Rome's great fire broke out in July 64 CE, adversaries accused Nero

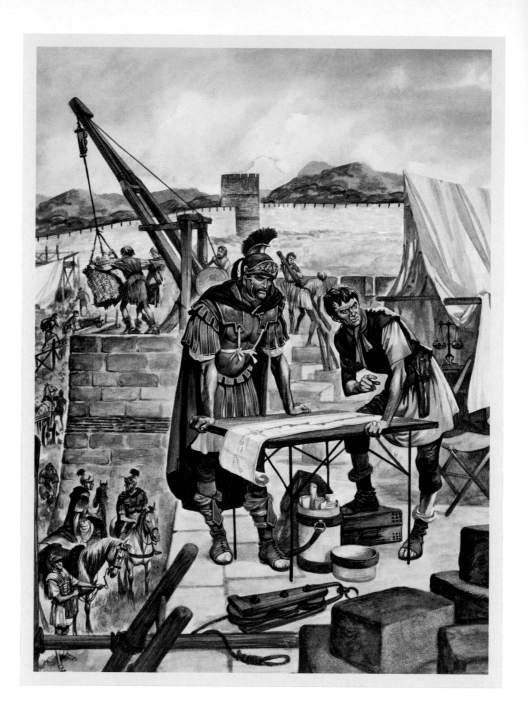

of setting it, claiming they had seen him playing the lyre and singing while Rome burned. The Senate eventually declared him a public enemy, and he took his own life.

After Nero's death, civil war erupted as senators competed for imperial authority. Vespasian finally prevailed, and he ruled from 69 to 79 CE. When his younger son, Domitian, assumed power in 81 CE, he alienated provincial governors. His insistence on being addressed as "Lord and God" reminded many of Nero. Domitian was murdered in 96 CE, and replaced with the elderly senator Nerva within hours.

Construction of the Colosseum in Rome was begun under Vespasian.

In addition to serving as emperor of Rome for almost 20 years, Marcus Aurelius was also a highly regarded philosopher.

Nerva served only two years but was the first of what became known as the Five Good Emperors. Rome embarked on nearly a century of unaccustomed stability. Under Nerva's successor, Trajan, Rome expanded its influence to more than 2.5 million square miles (6.5 million sq km). Senior equestrians, the social class second in prestige to the senators, were awarded important posts in imperial finance and correspondence. This helped to strengthen the emperor's relationship with Rome's elites.

Hadrian, Trajan's successor, promoted peace in imperial outposts and was an admirer of Greek culture. He supported several large public works projects and built aqueducts, baths, and theaters. Emperor Antoninus Pius continued his predecessor's policies and built numerous theaters and temples. Marcus Aurelius succeeded him in the year 161.

Soon afterward, northern tribes began to raid Rome. At the height of the raids, a smallpox **pandemic** struck Rome. At its

pandemic (pan-DEM-ik) an outbreak of disease that affects a very large region

worst, the plague killed more than two thousand Romans each day, weakening the imperial armed forces and complicating military defense. Perhaps between one-fourth and one-third of Rome's population died from smallpox between the years 165 and 180. While Marcus Aurelius was a superb leader, his son and successor, Commodus, abused imperial power and ignored his advisers. He was murdered in 192. Rome's golden age was at an end.

The following years saw an end to the peace of the previous ninety years. This period was marked by political turmoil, hostile family relationships, and violence. Emperor Caracalla was assassinated six years after he ordered the assassination of his co-emperor and younger brother, Geta. Emperor Elagabalus was tortured and thrown in the Tiber River. It was not until Alexander Severus became emperor in 222 that Rome saw a return to order and moderation. However, the growing strength of the Persian Empire threatened to plunge Rome into chaos once more.

Commodus is considered to have been a harsh and unfair ruler.

Alexander's assassination in 235 ushered in a host of problems. A succession of two dozen generals claimed the imperial throne over the course of the next half century, resulting in political chaos. Because generals were more interested in conquering new territories than defending imperial frontiers, foreign tribes raided the outskirts of the empire. Midcentury, the Roman army was drastically reduced by a plague of smallpox. The plague claimed as many as five thousand lives in a single day. The expense of defending the empire's crumbling frontiers brought Rome to the point of economic collapse and widespread civil disorder.

Between 258 and 260, Rome split into three states: a Roman Empire, centered in Italy; a Gallic Empire, composed of Hispania, Gaul, and Britannia; and the Palmyrene Empire, composed of Syria and Egypt. After becoming emperor in 284, Diocletian was able to reunite the empire and defeat the northern tribes threatening Rome. He instituted religious reforms, demanding that Christians in Rome give up their beliefs and follow the traditional Roman religion. He also began a new system where several emperors shared control of the empire.

Alexander Severus helped restore order to Rome after years of chaos, but was a weak military leader.

Following the end of Diocletian's reign in 305, Roman emperors began to reverse his religious reforms. In 313, the Edict of Milan officially proclaimed the toleration of Christianity in the Roman Empire. In 380, Emperor Theodosius I published the Edict

The ruins of a palace built by Diocletian still stand in modern-day Croatia.

Christianity became a major part of Roman culture during the fourth century CE.

of Thessalonica, adopting Christianity as the state religion of the Roman Empire.

The acceptance of Christianity in Rome had profound consequences for the history of Europe. It was also one of several factors contributing to the collapse of the Roman Empire in the west. Some historians argue that Christianity, which places more emphasis on the afterlife than our time on Earth, diminished the people's will to secure material blessings. Rome's coins were less valuable. Its military and political institutions were weakened. Rome did not work to develop colonial economies. Instead, it recklessly plundered its resources, turning colonies into slave economies.

Other historians and economists have suggested that the collapse of the empire was inevitable. As taxation in Rome increased, people moved to the countryside and became self-sufficient, sharply reducing tax revenues. The technological advances that had helped to propel Rome to dominance could not sustain its growth. Under increasing pressure from attacking tribes and suffering under the weight of failed economic policies, ancient Rome passed into history in the last quarter of the fifth century.

Emperors were responsible for issuing money in the form of precious metal coins, on which they put portraits of themselves and their relatives.

CHAPTER TWO

THE SHAPING OF ROMAN INSTITUTIONS

From the beginning, Rome's governmental institutions were shaped by social and economic forces. Rome responded to social change, including population increase and class

The Senate, an inheritance from the Republic, gradually became a valued ally of the emperors.

tensions between patricians and plebeians, by inventing new offices and changing the duties of existing offices. In Rome's early years, the king held almost all of the government's power. Only the Senate and the Curiate Assembly existed to check his powers. During the time of the republic, consuls had more limited powers than the king had possessed, since each checked the other. The republic also brought about the rise of a **hierarchy** of **magistrates**. In addition, a number of legislative assemblies enacted laws and tried cases. By the time of the Roman Empire, the legislative assemblies had grown weaker as the Senate's influence increased.

Patricians had many more advantages than the plebeians had.

hierarchy (HYE-ur-ahr-kee) an arrangement in which people or things have different ranks or levels of importance

magistrates (MAJ-i-strates) government officials who can act as judges in court

Thousands of years ago, nomads settled near the Tiber River in an area that would grow to become Rome.

veto (VEE-toh) forbid, or refuse to approve

THE RULE OF KINGS

Several centuries before Rome's legendary founding in 753 BCE, Indo-European nomads had settled in the hills east of the Tiber River. Older, more experienced men of the tribes held positions of leadership. Eventually, many tribes found it in their best interests to cooperate against invaders and trade with each other. They eventually formed the settlements that would grow to become Rome.

The Past Is Present
A GOVERNMENT AHEAD OF ITS TIME

The institutions that the Romans developed to administer the republic no longer exist, but the ideas underlying them are as important as ever. The U.S. government is based heavily on many of the ideas established during the Roman Republic.

The authors of the U.S. Constitution were especially influenced by an account of Rome's political structures written by the Greek historian Polybius. The U.S. government relies on a separation of powers between executive, legislative, and judicial branches. It is designed to include checks and balances that prevent any branch from becoming overly powerful.

The president may **veto** laws and appoint judges. The Supreme Court interprets laws passed by Congress. Congress (left) may override presidential vetoes. This system is very similar to the way plebeian legislative assemblies, aediles, and tribunes ensured that patrician institutions did not become too powerful.

Debates in the Roman Senate could be lively.

Consequently, early Roman institutions retained the **patriarchal** structure of the tribes. A group's leader, invariably an older male, resolved disputes and made decisions for the group as his clan's highest authority. The Roman Senate, in its earliest stages, was a coming together of these elders. Their numbers increased as the community grew. In all likelihood, the Senate existed prior to the establishment of the kingship. The Senate likely chose one member as its representative and invested supreme power in him. This position eventually developed into

patriarchal (pay-tree-ARK-uhl) led by males

that of king. The senators themselves, as heads of the community's prominent families, were Rome's original patricians.

The king held supreme power. The Senate could only approve of his decrees. The Senate lacked the power to issue decrees or make laws of its own. It was an advisory council to the king who

Assemblies made important decisions about local government issues.

The pontifex maximus was a key religious figure in ancient Roman society.

could, at his discretion, choose to ignore its advice. At the same time, the Senate informed the king of the community's desires. The Senate's influence grew only during the periods between one king's death and the election of his successor. During such times, senators exercised full leadership of the community.

Rome's Assembly possessed limited powers as well. Rome's three original tribes—Luceres, Ramnes, and Tities—were each separated into ten divisions, or *curiae*, comprised of the families living in a particular location. Curiae also served as the local unit of the Roman army. Each *curia* elected a spokesman for life. He was required to be at least fifty years old. These elected spokesmen formed the Curiate Assembly. It was the Assembly's responsibility to elect a new king after the Senate approved a nominee. The Assembly also played an important role in matters pertaining to family law. It was tasked with admitting new families to curiae and moving them from one curiae to another. In addition, the Assembly approved or denied adoptions and witnessed wills.

Another officer, the pontifex maximus, advised the king on religious matters, including religious rites, sacrifices, and burial of the dead. He was also charged with supervising religious funds and had authority over all religious institutions.

THE REPUBLIC AND SOCIAL CHANGE

Rome's constitution, founded on the ancient organizations of tribe and family, expanded and evolved in response to societal change. Though traditional custom persisted in the Roman Republic, the city-state's constitution evolved in response to social unrest, especially the struggle between its patrician founding families and ordinary citizens.

The revolution ending the era of monarchy caused two important changes. First, kingship was abandoned. In its place, two consuls were elected for one-year terms. Initially, the two consuls, acting together, had the same power as a king. In order for them to fully exercise that power, they needed to agree with each other. Each consul's power was limited both by his limited time in office and by the other consul. Consuls were military commanders and could summon the Senate or Assembly, but possessed less leadership in religious matters than kings had. These powers passed to the pontifex maximus and his subordinate, the *rex sacrorum*, a patrician who administered sacred rites and set the days of festivals.

Consuls gradually lost power as other magistrates were added to the government. By 442 BCE, consuls were stripped of their right to conduct the census. Two new officers, called censors, assumed the duty. The office of censor eventually became associated with regulation of public morality. Censors also assumed

Praetors presided over a variety of legal issues.

a leading role in government finance until the office was finally eliminated in 22 BCE.

The office of praetor may have been created to hear cases of law, and often had religious duties. Eventually, as the republic grew through conquest, more praetors were added to act as provincial governors. By the time of Julius Caesar, there were sixteen praetors in the Roman government.

In the republic's early days, the Senate and Assemblies had little power. In 509 BCE, some plebeians were made senators, but they lacked many of the powers of their patrician colleagues. The plebeians **seceded** in 494 BCE, while Rome battled with two neighboring tribes. To avert catastrophe, patricians gave in to their demands. Plebeians could, for the first time, elect officials in their own assembly.

Conflict between the plebeians and the patricians eventually led to more governmental positions for the plebeians.

Tribunes helped make sure that the government did not stand in the way of the rights of the common people.

The office of plebeian tribune was created, and there were originally two tribunes. They possessed considerable authority, and could summon the Plebeian Council and enforce its decrees. Eventually, they grew in influence and could veto acts of the magistrates. This conflict between plebeians and patricians continued to direct the evolution of government in Rome. Many of Rome's wealthy citizens, lacking patrician roots, began to look to the Plebeian Council as a way to dismantle the patricians' exclusive power.

In 367 BCE, further concessions were made. Plebeians were made eligible to become consuls. Twenty-five years later, it was further established that one of Rome's two consuls must be a plebeian. By 339 BCE, the same rule was extended to the selection of censors. In 300 BCE, further legislation allowed plebeians to become priests. As the class struggle deepened, the plebeians continued to gain concessions until 287 BCE when a set of laws made the Plebeian Council's resolutions binding on all of the people of Rome.

Plebeians were first allowed to become priests in 300 BCE.

Another office, aedile, had been created at the same time as that of plebeian tribune. Aediles protected the common people, oversaw cult practices, and were in charge of the water supply. They were also involved in the regulation of markets and the distribution of Rome's corn supply. Aediles and plebeian tribunes helped safeguard the liberties of Rome's common people by acting as a check on the power of the patrician Senate.

Assemblies and councils held a variety of different powers. The Assembly of the Curia could confirm appointment of magistrates, witness wills, and preside over adoptions throughout the era of the republic. Initially, it passed laws and tried judicial cases, but the Assembly of the Centuries gradually absorbed those powers. This Assembly could declare war, elect consuls and censors, and enact laws. The Assembly's 193 *centuriae* were divided among the five wealth classes in ways that gave Rome's wealthiest citizens more influence and its poorest ones none at all. A Tribal Assembly was organized on the basis of geographical location. This assembly elected aediles and plebeian tribunes, held trials, and enacted resolutions.

The assemblies were never truly democratic institutions. People in the city of Rome made up only four of Rome's thirty-five tribes, and those living far from the city were usually unable to attend meetings. This gave more power to people living in the city. However, the legislative assemblies demonstrated a refined understanding of checks and balances. The Assembly of the Centuries elected censors, who in turn could add new senators or remove existing ones. Senators could direct censors and consuls. The Plebeian Council elected tribunes and aediles, who could veto the acts of the Senate or any assembly.

Standing on the World Stage

Assemblies, so important in the Roman Republic, lost almost all of their power after Caesar's assassination. The geographical expansion of the empire made assemblies and councils, designed for local service, obsolete. Instead, power was invested in the Senate. Senators were required to have wealth equivalent to 12,000 aurei. The aureus, a gold coin, had a weight of about 8 grams (0.28 ounces), but was later reduced in size and purity. Consequently, senators needed to possess the equivalent of 220 pounds (100 kilograms) of pure gold.

After the murder of Caesar, assemblies ceased to be an important part of the Roman legislative process.

Because the power of assemblies now rested in the hands of the Senate, the Senate's decrees were law. The Senate could enact tax laws, but only with the agreement of the emperor. It could try criminal cases and cases involving treason acting as the jury, and hand down verdicts. Even then, the emperor reserved the right to veto any ruling. The presumed balance of power between the Senate and the emperor was no balance at all. Increasingly, the emperor asserted his right to ignore the conclusions of senators. He gradually gained uncontested power to declare war and approve treaties.

The checks and balances of the republic vanished as the assemblies and councils that were representative of the popular will were

The Senate was the most powerful government institution during the early days of the empire.

absorbed into the Senate. The Senate, in turn, gradually gave up its powers to the emperor and the offices he created. It became a crime punishable by death to even speak poorly of the emperor. In turn, the emperor could order anyone put to death for any reason he desired. Emperors also assumed many of the powers delegated to censors during the era of the republic. An emperor could now conduct the census and oversee matters of public morality. The emperor had ultimate rule over the military and assumed the powers of pontifex maximus, allowing him to control state religion.

Emperors had the final say in all legal matters.

CHAPTER THREE

LAND OF DESTINY

The earliest Romans believed their city was founded on a spot chosen by the gods. What is more certain is that it was one favored by nature. Steep cliffs flank the Tiber River basin at Rome. **Tributaries** of the Tiber carved out the Seven Hills of Rome, where the earliest villages were formed.

The Apennine Mountains were difficult to cross, and therefore helped prevent potential threats from reaching Rome.

The river snakes its way through the valley. At one turn, the Tiber is relatively shallow and splits its course at an island. This **ford** is the only place in the valley where the Tiber could be easily crossed. Surrounded by hills and outcroppings, the area was easily defended to the west. The Apennine Mountains, which run lengthwise through Italy, made the river ford inaccessible from the east. The Alps to the north formed a barrier against invasion during the winter months, their passes buried under deep snow except in the warmest of winters. The Tiber ford was also ideal for traders crossing the river and for migrating tribes.

The Alps stretch about 750 miles (1,207 km) across several European nations.

tributaries (TRIB-yuh-ter-eez) streams that flow into larger streams, rivers, or lakes

ford (FORD) a shallow part of a stream or river where it can be crossed

The Past Is Present
STANDING THE TEST OF TIME

In addition to making soil fertile, volcanic eruptions in central Italy deposited a fine volcanic ash in the area. Early Romans found that this ash could be combined with lime and water to make strong and durable concrete. However, it took a very long time for them to perfect the process. The development of concrete resulted in an architectural revolution. Massive public works projects—baths, aqueducts, amphitheaters, temples, dams, and domes—became more common by the end of the republic and throughout the imperial era. Some of these concrete structures have stood the test of time for two thousand years. Today, we continue to use updated versions of this incredible building material in a wide variety of construction projects, from driveways and parking lots to enormous buildings and bridges.

Rome was born on the hilltops surrounding the ford. Archaeologists place the earliest settlement atop the Palatine Hill. They have found evidence of an isolated village of thatched huts that existed since before 1000 BCE. Ancient tools and pots have been unearthed there. Settlements also have been found on the flat-topped Esquiline and Quirinal Hills.

The river valley itself was marshy and was not drained until the construction of the Cloaca Maxima. Rome's Forum was built there as the small hilltop villages began cooperating with one another. Volcanoes also played an important role in the history of Rome. The Italian Peninsula contains fourteen volcanoes. Ancient eruptions left

The ruins below Palatine Hill are among Rome's most popular tourist attractions.

summers and cold, wet winters. On the eastern down slopes of the Apennines, hot, dry winds create a desolate environment in summer. In winter, northeastern winds make northern parts of this region colder than those west of the Apennines.

The Mediterranean climate of the rest of the peninsula consists essentially of two seasons: one wet and mild, and the other dry and hot. Although agricultural production varied from region to region during ancient times, the area around Rome—dominated by medium-size farms—grew grapes, olives, wheat, barley, and a variety of vegetables and fruits. Great amounts of wheat were also grown in the Po Valley.

The ruins of this ancient theater stand near the modern city of Florence.

Other locations with suitable climates for agriculture and favorable geography became major centers in ancient Rome. The city of Florence was born in the Arno River basin, surrounded by hills. Its location on the Via Cassia established it as a major trade center. Genoa, at the northern end of the Via Cassia, thrived because of its deep harbor. Etruscans, Phoenicians, Greeks, and Romans occupied the area at various times. Mild climate and fertile soil spurred the growth of Naples. Naples was originally a settlement in Magna Graecia, the Greek colonies of southern Italy. Magna Graecia became part of the Roman Republic in the third century BCE.

Today, Naples is one of the largest cities in Italy.

As the Roman Empire expanded, more land became available for agriculture.

THE MIXED BLESSINGS OF EMPIRE

The Italian Peninsula has far fewer harbors than the nearby Balkan Peninsula. As a result, the Roman Empire's opportunities for overseas trade depended, to an extent, on gaining access to the natural harbors ringing the Mediterranean Sea. Rome's expansion during the imperial age solved this issue. It also provided land for a growing population, helped to relieve class tensions arising from unequal land distribution, and expanded Rome's natural resources and wealth. Rome conquered and annexed Sicily (241 BCE), Sardinia and Corsica (238 BCE), Spain (197 BCE), Macedonia and regions of northern Africa (146 BCE), and parts of Asia Minor (133 BCE) in the late republic. Expansion proceeded at a faster rate under the empire. At its peak, Rome controlled all of the land ringing the Mediterranean basin, Gaul, Britain, Asia Minor, and Syria. It also established trade routes to Asia.

Besides providing a base for taxation, conquered lands provided ports and agricultural resources. Only one-fifth of the Italian Peninsula consisted of plains that could be cultivated. The Alps and Apennines comprised half of the remainder, with the rest covered in larger hills and forests. The geographical resources of the Mediterranean basin provided additional lands for growing dietary staples—grains, grapes, and olives—for the people of the empire.

To facilitate trade with East Africa, Rome exploited the ports at Arsinoe, on the Gulf of Suez, and Myos Hormos and Berenice, on the Red Sea. The empire also entered into agreements for safe transportation of corn from Africa and Egypt. Roman imperial expansion brought wealth and opportunities for maritime trade that the few natural harbors of the Italian Peninsula could not offer. It also brought the smallpox pandemic that worsened the crisis of the third century. In addition, the relative ease of travel allowed new religions, such as Christianity, to spread into Rome.

CHAPTER FOUR

BOUND BY TRADITION

en dominated family life in ancient Rome. The family's
oldest living male, the paterfamilias, traditionally held
absolute power over his wife, children, adopted children,

Members of ancient Roman families were raised to obey the man of the house.

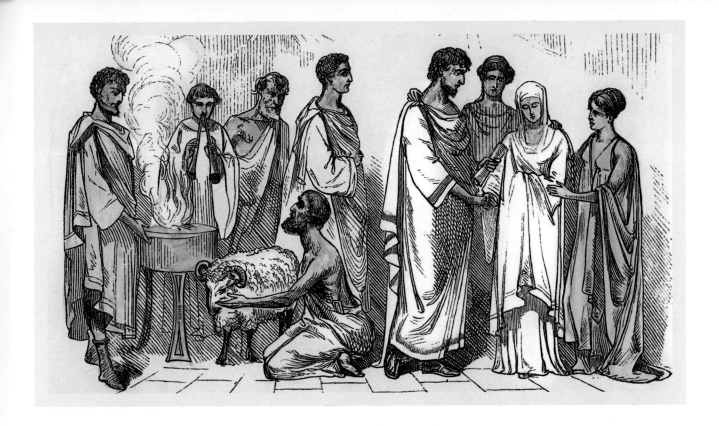

and slaves. He was expected to maintain ancestral customs and Rome's time-honored code of moral conduct within his family. He honored his clan's ancestral gods and participated in Rome's political and religious institutions, setting an example of citizenship for members of his household. The power of the paterfamilias, *patria potestas*, also extended over his sons' children. Each family could have only one paterfamilias. When a young man reached adulthood, he was not a paterfamilias until his father died or chose to free him. Patria potestas could be terminated under a few specific conditions, such as if the son or sons were adopted by a new family or if the paterfamilias became insane.

When a son married, his wife was also placed under his father's power. If a daughter wished to marry, she could not do

Traditionally, weddings brought the bride under the control of the groom's paterfamilias.

so without her father's consent. The power of the paterfamilias was terrifying and absolute. Adult children could be banished or executed on his command. Traitorous sons or daughters could be certain of their fate. Newborns fared no better. After being born, they were placed on the ground. If the paterfamilias picked the child up, he or she was taken into the clan. If not, he or she was abandoned. Sons and daughters could own no property of their own, but only care for property belonging to the paterfamilias, with his permission.

A paterfamilias had the power to decide whether or not a woman was allowed to keep her newborn baby.

The Past Is Present
THAT'S ENTERTAINMENT

The gladiatorial contests, chariot races, and other events held in Rome's various stadiums, theaters, and amphitheaters were popular sources of entertainment for the ancient Romans. At the height of the Roman Empire, tens of thousands of people would pack the seats of these ancient theaters to take in a thrilling spectacle. The Romans built hundreds of these massive entertainment structures. The ruins of many of these structures still stand today.

Roman theaters and stadiums have been a major influence on modern entertainment venues. Today's football stadiums and racetracks look remarkably similar to the ruins of ancient Roman amphitheaters. Like the ancient Romans, many people today love to visit these massive structures to watch exciting sporting events and enjoy other forms of public entertainment.

Women had little power. They could neither hold political office nor vote. However, the legal status of women improved by the late republic. Even in the early republic, some women owned land and composed their own wills. Others were skillful orators and represented themselves in court. Though it was custom that daughters would always be loyal to their fathers, married women had more freedom. A daughter continued to have the same relationship to her father under Roman law after marrying, but she lived separately with her husband and saw her father less often. Many aristocratic women were married by age fourteen and were expected to provide their husbands with children.

By the late republic, aristocratic women, who could possess property, were very involved in business transactions. Many had grown less interested in traditional motherhood, which had existed during previous centuries. Consequently, aristocratic birthrates declined, even

Just as they are today, weddings in ancient Rome were considered highly important, sacred events.

as the slave population was expanding. The first Roman emperor, Augustus, was so alarmed by this that he passed laws granting important privileges to women who had at least three children.

A woman's role could be exceptionally demanding. An aristocratic woman was expected to manage a large household, but she had slaves who did most of the routine labor. Aristocratic women were often responsible for educating their children. Women whose husbands governed provinces might have to take full command of several estates and hundreds of slaves for years, making all of the husband's social and business decisions in his absence. Plebeian women might be **midwives**, dancers, or secretaries. Others

Women were responsible for supervising the family's children.

midwives (MID-wyves) people who are trained to help women give birth

Children often amused themselves by playing games.

prepared food for sale. Weaving was a skill that was expected of all women, regardless of social standing.

Children played several games that exist to this day, though in slightly altered forms. Boys played a variety of ball games and leapfrog. They also enjoyed knucklebones, a game similar to jacks, except sheep knuckles were used. Girls played with dolls, about 6 inches (15 centimeters) tall, made of ivory and bone. Public games, *ludi*, were a regular part of Roman life. Chariot racing, gladiatorial contests, great feasts, and parades were held at Rome's

Circus Maximus. By imperial times, more than one-third of the calendar was devoted to these public spectacles.

Education played an important role in the Roman family. In patrician circles, boys were prepared for public life and military service. Plebeian boys were trained for lives as farmers and merchants. Mothers readied their daughters for domestic life. Gradually, reading and writing became a more important part of education. By the second century BCE, Rome had more extensive contact with Greek civilization and began to adopt its educational practices. Greek tutors educated the children of patrician families. Elementary schools for both boys and girls opened in the third century BCE.

Older children learned Latin grammar and poetry from qualified teachers, though these educators did not appear often before the second century BCE. Children of the wealthier classes completed their education with a rhetor. Rhetors taught Greek standards of effective speaking.

The Clothes Make the Man (and Woman)

Roman clothing was most often made of wool, with underclothing made of linen. Roman women wore the *palla*, a large, rectangular piece of cloth that could be draped in a variety of ways. Women of the patrician class also wore silk.

Originally, both men and women wore togas, long cloths that were wrapped around the body. However, by the second century BCE, the toga came to be an almost exclusively male garment. Fashioned from a semicircular cloth, it could only be worn by Roman citizens. The toga was worn over a linen tunic, which resembled a long shirt that hung to a point between the hips and ankles.

The tunic was worn for agricultural labor because it allowed freedom of movement. Senators and consuls wore tunics while plowing their fields or relaxing indoors, but put on togas when receiving visitors or appearing in public. It was considered improper to appear in the Roman Forum or at public games without a toga.

The palla was a common garment worn by ancient Roman women.

Over time, togas grew in size and variety, and became a marker of social status. Eventually, they came to be more than 20 feet (6 m) long. The center of the toga, held beneath the right arm, was draped backward and forward over the left shoulder. When boys reached age fourteen, they wore the *toga virilis*, a plain white toga that stood as a sign of their maturity. Before age fourteen, they wore the *toga praetexta*, bordered by a purple stripe. Rome's monarchs, priests, and augurs wore togas with a similar design. Men seeking public office wore the bleached white *toga candida*. Consequently, we still call people seeking political office candidates. By the imperial age, generals wore the *toga picta*, a

Togas were made in a variety of colors and styles.

gold-embroidered, solid purple toga, in triumphal processions at the Circus Maximus. Mourners wore dark togas. Military men also wore cloaks, traditionally pinned at the right shoulder. Two types, the Celtic *sagum* and *paludamentum*, were rectangular, while the *chlamys* was fashioned as a semicircle, not unlike the toga.

Though Roman women dressed simply, they adorned themselves with jewelry. They wore necklaces, rings, and earrings of emerald and pearl, and also precious metals. Women applied chalk to whiten their faces and crimson makeup to blush their cheeks. They routinely dyed their hair and applied lead-based eyeliner. Increasingly, a long, pleated dress called a *stola* became the standard attire for older women.

Senators and other elected officials wore plain white togas.

A PLACE OF THEIR OWN

Roman houses varied considerably with time period, location, and the owners' social standing. The houses of aristocrats consisted of a central hall, the atrium, with rooms surrounding it. The center ceiling of the atrium opened to the sky. In the earliest houses, the **hearth** was located in the atrium. Later, the atrium was likely to contain only the clan's collection of funeral masks, to honor ancestors, and a small shrine to guardian household **deities**. Bedrooms led directly off the atrium, along with a dining room and a study. Agricultural products were sold in the house's *taberna*, a shop where a number of services or prepared foods might also be

Ancient Romans wore their finest clothing to theater performances and other public events.

hearth (HARTH) fireplace used for cooking in ancient Roman homes

deities (DEE-i-teez) gods or goddesses

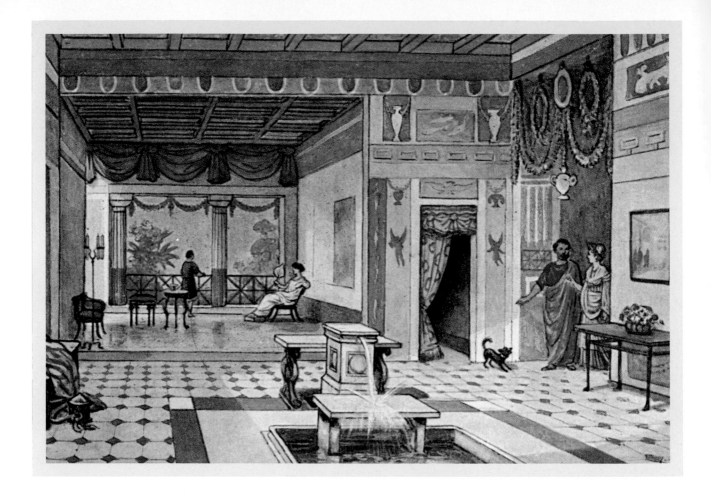

Wealthy Romans lived in large, elaborately decorated homes.

purchased. With sufficient room to expand, the wealthy combined basic designs with elaborate columns, courts, and gardens. The houses in the city of Pompeii, many built by the first century BCE, show this classic design.

The eruption of Mount Vesuvius in 79 CE completely buried Pompeii. Excavations that have taken place since its rediscovery in 1748 reveal a city modeled on a grand scale in the second and first centuries BCE. Spectacular fountains, theaters, an amphitheater, and elaborate homes have been excavated. The streets, laid out in close-fitting stones, form a regular grid. Larger homes in Pompeii, such as the remarkable House of the Faun, have enlarged atria, many bedrooms and corridors, private baths, and kitchens. There are also dining rooms, parlors for greeting guests, and studies.

Few Romans could afford such incredible homes. City dwellers seldom had their own property. Instead, they rented space from the wealthy. Eventually, some upper-class citizens began to build entire blocks of simple but affordable housing for Rome's ordinary citizens. These *insulae*, multistory brick structures, varied in quality and housed all but the wealthiest citizens. Ancient Rome, though united by common beliefs and customs, was divided by differences in wealth and status, which were marked by homes and clothing.

The discovery at Pompeii provided researchers with new insight into how the ancient Romans lived.

CHAPTER FIVE

DO AS THE ROMANS DO

Romulus and the deity Quirinus were believed to be one and the same.

From Rome's beginning, home life, religious practice, and government were interwoven to a great extent. Romulus, Rome's legendary first king, is said to have used powers of augury to learn the will of the gods when he founded Rome on the Palatine Hill. Thus, the Romans believed that their city was built according to the wishes of the gods. The death of Romulus is not recorded. Instead, he disappears mysteriously, only to be resurrected as the god Quirinus centuries later. A festival called the Quirinalia, held each year on February 17, commemorated his role as protector of the early Roman state, and an altar dedicated to Quirinus was erected on the Quirinal Hill, northeast of the city center.

The atrium of each Roman home contained statues of Lares, which were household deities and protectors of family, home, and fields. Other household deities, called Penates, were associated with Aeneas's escape from Troy and his role in founding Rome. Penates were also linked to Vesta, the goddess of the hearth.

Lares were gods of homes and families.

The Past Is Present
PICTURE PERFECT

The ancient Romans were among the first people to paint realistic portraits of people. While other cultures had created representations of humans, they had not generally attempted to create art that captured the appearance of specific individuals. During the Republican era ancient Roman families began hanging portraits of notable ancestors in their homes, just as people today decorate their walls, tables, and desks with photographs of friends and relatives. During the time of the Empire, countless statues, busts, and coins were created to depict

members of the imperial family. Similarly, statues, paintings, and photographs of world leaders are a common sight in the public spaces of many modern countries.

In addition to worshipping these deities of the home, ancient Romans also participated in public cults. A public cult worshipping the Penates was established at the Forum's ancient Temple of Vesta. Thus, Vesta was worshipped both at home and in public ceremonies. A broad range of Lares, each one protector of a specific domain, also had public cults.

Romans celebrated more than three dozen religious festivals each year, many of which lasted for several days. As a result, there were more days with religious festivals than without. Festivals were held in honor of a broad range of deities. Some, such as the Compitalia held in honor of the Lares, were very ancient. During the Compitalia, wool figures of a household's inhabitants were hung beside doors as an offering to Mania, goddess of the dead. Some festivals included street theater, acrobatics, and chariot racing. Others were solemn religious observances.

Military success in ancient Rome was attributed to a combination of divine favor and human virtue. Before major

Vesta was worshipped as the goddess of the hearth.

As the god of war, Mars was one of the most important deities in the Roman pantheon.

battles, military camps sacrificed rams, bulls, and boars to the gods. Because the ceremony forged a connection between the camp and the gods, victory in battle was believed to be a sign of the gods' approval of the Roman cause. Triumphant generals wore the toga picta and rode through the streets of Rome in chariots. Monuments were erected to celebrate them, and coins were sometimes minted in their honor.

The expansion of Rome during the republican and imperial ages brought the Romans into direct contact with other cultures, each with its own religious traditions. A combination of military conquest, treaties, and trade added to the large and ever growing Roman **pantheon**. As contact with Greece grew, the worship of Greek deities became common in Rome. Roman gods quickly inherited much of the Greek gods' rich mythology. Consequently, many gods of the Roman pantheon have familiar Greek counterparts. For example, Mars was equated with Ares, Diana with Artemis, and Venus with Aphrodite. The vast Roman Empire incorporated the cults of civilizations it conquered, rejecting very few.

Acceptance of foreign religions was not universal. During the early days of the empire, Christianity was feared as a source of social disruption. Because it rejected traditional Roman religious practices, it appealed to the poor living at the fringes of the empire with little stake in Rome's continued success. Some emperors, such as Nero, blamed any Christians for problems that occurred. Some emperors even ordered the destruction of Christian churches. But Christianity prevailed against all odds, winning the approval of the empire in 380 CE as official support for all other cults was withdrawn. When the Western Empire collapsed less than a century later, Christianity was the only religion to survive.

The spread of Christianity eventually led to the end of traditional Roman religion.

Trajan's Column still stands today.

COLUMNS, ARCHES, AQUEDUCTS, AND DOMES

Rome's art, history, and religious beliefs blend in magnificent public works and massive displays of triumph and imperial power. Trajan's Column and pedestal, built near the Quirinal Hill in Rome, reaches a height of 125 feet (38 m). Completed in 113 CE to celebrate imperial victory over the Dacians and the annexation of Dacia—a kingdom spanning the Carpathian Mountains of central and eastern Europe—the column brings together a number of Roman themes.

Trajan's Column contains an interior spiral staircase, a Greek innovation. Its exterior is magnificently carved with a **frieze** stretching from bottom to top, recording the exploits of the imperial army in its war against the Dacians. Realistic depictions of battle scenes, weapons, ships, and fortifications provide historians with a glimpse into Rome's military operations at the opening of the second century.

Besides grand triumphal art, Romans valued such works as ivory carvings and glass figurines. Red-gloss pottery embellished with reliefs of agricultural deities was used for serving dinner guests. Plain pottery, coarse in construction, was used for food preparation. The Romans also prized engraved gemstones and distinctive, ring-mounted seals, which were used by emperors to press one-of-a-kind designs into hardened wax as a mark of identification.

Fine miniature paintings were used to illustrate religious texts. A number of unusual substances were used to add color to these illuminated manuscripts. Red coloring was made from insect larvae and rust. Black coloring came from charcoal, and yellow from turmeric, a common spice. Earwax and urine were important components of several colors.

Beginning no later than the early first century CE, realistic portraits of mummies began to appear west of the Nile. In the

This illuminated manuscript depicts a scene from Virgil's Aeneid.

Al Fayyum Oasis, the wealthy commissioned realistic funeral masks. Similar masks were displayed in the atria of Roman houses and became an important part of religious festivals commemorating dead ancestors. By the middle of the third century CE, the empire's economic crisis put the cost of funeral art out of reach of all but the wealthiest aristocrats, and the practice vanished.

However meaningful these art objects were to the Romans themselves, it is the grand public works—columns, arches, aqueducts, and domes—that continue to inspire awe. The precision of the Pantheon's massive dome, the grace of the Bridge of Tiberius, and the ingenuity of the Pont du Gard aqueduct bridge in southern France show the genius of Roman engineers. The perfection of Roman concrete, coupled with two centuries of relative peace and imperial prosperity, fostered an architectural revolution between 27 BCE and 180 CE. Amphitheaters, fountains, and public baths were among the other incredible structures created by Roman engineers.

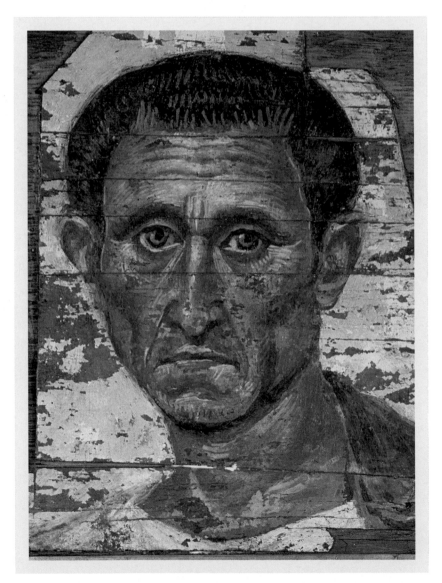

Funeral portraits were popular during the first and second centuries CE.

These engineers depended on their Greek predecessors for inspiration and technical expertise. By expanding on the Greeks' ideas, they pushed the boundary of architecture to heights previously unimagined. Roman engineers adopted Greek Doric, Ionic, and Corinthian designs in their creations, but also developed their own distinctive variations. Roman artists embraced the genius of the Greek author Homer and produced illuminated manuscripts of his work. Roman culture, in all aspects, evolved by embracing the traditions of trading partners and conquered people. A culture defined by unending thirst for expansion could hardly have developed otherwise.

The Pont du Gard stands as an excellent example of the ancient Romans' amazing engineering abilities.

CHAPTER SIX

MONUMENTS AND MEMORIES

A succession of military reversals, economic crises, and pandemics all pointed toward an unavoidable collapse for the Roman Empire. The defeat of the Roman army by Germanic rebels at the Battle of Adrianople in 378 CE revealed how vulnerable the imperial military had become. There were

The Roman emperor Valens died at the Battle of Adrianople.

many reasons for its decline. A succession of pandemics had greatly reduced Rome's population. This not only thinned the army directly, but also weakened the tax base needed to support it. The empire responded by taxing Rome's citizens heavily. Many fled the city to settle in the countryside and become farmers.

Rome's weakened military was unable to prevail against attacks by wandering tribes. After the catastrophe of Adrianople, Rome was forced to hire some tribes to fight the others, opening the empire to the divided loyalties of a **mercenary** army. The presence of mercenaries in Roman outposts led to unnecessary confrontations and occasional riots. Confrontations between Roman authorities and tribes living within their boundaries grew worse when Emperor Theodosius I named Christianity the empire's sole religion, outlawing other religions.

Theodosius I declared a permanent end to the traditional Roman religion.

mercenary (MUR-suh-ner-ee) hired soldier

The Vandals fought their way into Rome, leaving destruction in their wake.

In 405 CE, in the depths of winter, the Rhine River froze. Iranian and Germanic tribes poured over the frozen river into Gaul. The Roman military could not force them back. The tribes soon extended their influence into both Hispania and Africa. Five years later, Visigoth tribes sacked Rome. By 455 CE, Rome could not resist the invasion of Vandal tribes, and it was sacked for a second time. The invasion of Italy by the East Germanic general Odoacer in 476 CE sounded the death knell for the Roman Empire in the west.

Historians have worked tirelessly to understand the reasons for the empire's collapse. Some place the blame primarily on the spread of Christianity. However, the Eastern Roman Empire, more economically stable than the Western Roman Empire, survived nearly a thousand years after the west's collapse—even though Christianity was better established in the east. Some historians, pointing to the waves of smallpox that weakened the empire, see Rome's shrinking population as the main reason for its demise. Disease weakened the army directly and shrank the tax base, making military funding more difficult. Rising taxes caused social unrest and an exodus from the city to the countryside.

The Past Is Present
A LASTING LANGUAGE

Latin, the official language of the Roman Empire in the west, outlived Rome because of its adoption by the Catholic Church. As a result, French, Spanish, Italian, Portuguese, Romanian, and dozens of other modern languages have their roots in Latin. From the fifth through the tenth centuries, Latin developed differently in different regions as it mixed with local terms and ways of speaking. These changes slowed with the development of the printing press, which standardized spelling and grammar to an extent. By then, the legacy of Rome's language was woven through the tongues of most of

Europe. When the Normans invaded England in 1066, countless French and Latin phrases made their way into the language. Today, more than half of the words in the English language come from Latin. The very words on this page are written using the Latin alphabet, which has become the most widely used alphabet in the world.

The picture that emerges from close examination of the western empire is a complex one. A lethal combination of economic trouble, military failures, pandemics, civil wars, and Germanic invasions spelled the end of the empire in the west. In the east, the empire lived on a millennium after the collapse in Rome. Its survival preserved Greco-Roman culture long after it disappeared in Western Europe.

AN EVER-PRESENT LEGACY

Many times each day, we encounter the legacy of ancient Rome, often without recognizing what we see and hear. These gifts shape the world, and are as common and ever present as the air we breathe. The Roman Catholic Church played a key role in the preservation of the Latin language and memories of Rome. Through Christianity, aspects of Roman culture were spread to areas outside the Roman Empire. Christian communities preserved ancient Roman writings and art. Their missionaries traveled to northern Europe, carrying Roman traditions with them. The church integrated the practices of Roman law into its religious laws, thereby preserving the spirit and structure of the Roman legal system for centuries.

Rome's architectural grandeur survives in today's U.S. Capitol. The building's massive fresco painting, *The Apotheosis of Washington*, depicts America's first president set among Roman gods and goddesses. The Jefferson Memorial, Washington Monument, White House, and New York's Washington Square Arch are all are based on Rome's rich architectural tradition.

It is easy to overlook the influence of ancient Rome in our daily lives. Yet, the national symbols, language, and religion of the

United States and many other modern societies are all founded on beliefs and practices that survived the Roman Empire. Our commitment to justice owes something to Rome, our political institutions even more. Our understanding of family, most of the words we use when we speak, and our traditional values as a culture are Roman. Though Rome's empire disappeared more than fifteen hundred years ago, its legacy will likely last far into the future.

The Apotheosis of Washington *is painted on the interior of the dome in the U.S. Capitol Building.*

BIOGRAPHIES

JULIUS **CAESAR** (100–44 BCE) was a brilliant military strategist and a strong leader at the end of the Roman Republic. Declared dictator for life, he was feared by several of the senators, who plotted his assassination. His murder, surely one of the defining historical events of ancient Rome, initiated a period of bloody civil war and imperial expansion that revolutionized Roman culture.

CONSTANTINE I (CA. 280–337 CE) was the first of Rome's emperors to convert to Christianity. He reclaimed some of Dacia for the empire and renamed the Greek colony of Byzantium Constantinople.

MARCUS AURELIUS (121–180 CE), emperor from 161 to 180, was a superb leader and statesman. He successfully fought against Persia's Parthian Empire, as well as the Sarmatians of Scythia. However, he is now better remembered for his *Meditations*, a collection of philosophic writings.

Nero (37–68 CE) was emperor from the years 54 to 68. He cared little for the Roman military, instead focusing on Greek culture and grandiose building projects such as the Golden House. When the city burned in the year 64, some blamed the fire on Nero, saying he had set it to clear land for his new palace. Nero blamed it on the Christians.

Servius Tullius (REIGNED 578–535 BCE) was Rome's sixth king and a champion of the plebeians. He initiated the Roman census, established the Century Assembly modeled on the Roman army, built a new wall around Rome, and established the Compitalia festival.

Tarquin THE ELDER (REIGNED 616–578 BCE) was the fifth king of Rome, according to legend. He is credited with building the Cloaca Maxima and Circus Maximus, as well as a stone wall around Rome. Before his assassination, he increased Rome's wealth and prestige and began the annexation of nearby cities.

Theodosius I (347–395 CE) published the Edict of Thessalonica in the year 380, adopting Christianity as the state religion of the Roman Empire.

Trajan (53–117 CE) was emperor of Rome from the years 98 to 117. He waged war against Dacia, Arabia, and Parthia and expanded the size of the empire. He pushed massive rebuilding projects in Rome that changed the city in fundamental ways.

TIMELINE

578 BCE: *Servius Tullius becomes king.*

1000 BCE: *Bronze Age settlements are constructed on Palatine Hill.*

600 BCE: *The Cloaca Maxima is built.*

616 BCE: *Tarquin the Elder becomes king.*

642 BCE: *Ancus Marcius is elevated to kingship.*

1000 BCE

750 BCE

672 BCE: *Tullus Hostilius succeeds Numa.*

715 BCE: *Numa becomes the second king of Rome.*

753 BCE: *Rome is founded by Romulus.*

535 BCE:
Servius is assassinated in the streets of Rome.

509 BCE:
Beginning of the Roman Republic.

494 BCE:
Plebeians secede from Rome.

222 BCE:
The Po Valley is brought under Roman dominion.

March 15, 44 BCE:
Julius Caesar is assassinated.

March 27 BCE:
Beginning of the Roman Empire

500 BCE

250 BCE

339 BCE:
Plebeians gain the right to be elevated to the office of censor.

367 BCE:
Plebeians gain the right to be elevated to the office of consul.

449 BCE:
Patricians grant the Plebeian Council the right to pass general resolutions.

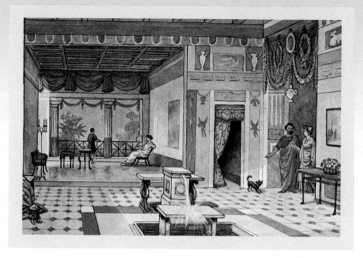

258–260 CE:
*The Roman Empire
splits into three parts.*

| 0 | 100 CE | 200 CE |

79 CE:
*Eruption of
Mount Vesuvius*

64 CE:
Great Fire of Rome

410 CE:
The Visigoths sack Rome.

476 CE:
The empire falls in the west.

300 CE   **400 CE**   **500 CE**

380 CE:
*The Edict of Thessalonica proclaims
Christianity as the official state religion.*

378 CE:
*The Roman military is
defeated at Adrianople.*

313 CE:
*The Edict of Milan
promotes religious tolerance
as imperial policy.*

GLOSSARY

ambassador (am-BAS-uh-dor) official sent by a government to represent it in another country

annexing (AN-eks-ing) taking control of a country or territory by force

aristocratic (uh-riss-tuh-KRAT-ik) belonging to the upper social classes

census (SEN-suhs) an official count of all the people living in a country or district

consuls (KAHN-suhlz) high-ranking officials of the Roman government

decrees (di-KREEZ) official decisions or orders

deities (DEE-i-teez) gods or goddesses

ford (FORD) a shallow part of a stream or river where it can be crossed

frieze (FREEZ) decorative band

hearth (HARTH) fireplace used for cooking in ancient Roman homes

hegemony (heh-JEH-muh-nee) strong cultural or economic influence of a dominant group

hereditary (huh-RED-i-ter-ee) passed from parent to child

hierarchy (HYE-ur-ahr-kee) an arrangement in which people or things have different ranks or levels of importance

latifundia (la-ti-FOON-dee-uh) extremely large areas of land that are usually used to grow crops for profit

legislator (LEJ-is-lay-tur) official with the power to make or change laws

magistrates (MAJ-i-strates) government officials who can act as judges in court

mercenary (MUR-suh-ner-ee) hired soldier

midwives (MID-wyves) people who are trained to help women give birth

pandemic (pan-DEM-ik) an outbreak of disease that affects a very large region

pantheon (PAN-thee-ahn) the gods of a particular mythology grouped together

patriarchal (pay-tree-ARK-uhl) led by males

patrician (puh-TRIH-shun) a member of one of the noble families of ancient Rome

pious (PYE-uhs) practicing a religion faithfully and seriously

plebeians (pli-BEE-uhnz) the common people of ancient Rome

republic (ri-PUHB-lik) a form of government in which the people have the power to elect representatives who manage the government

seceded (si-SEED-id) formally withdrew from a group or an organization

toga (TOH-guh) a piece of clothing worn by people in ancient Rome; it was wrapped around the body and draped over the left shoulder

tributaries (TRIB-yuh-ter-eez) streams that flow into larger streams, rivers, or lakes

veto (VEE-toh) forbid, or refuse to approve

FIND OUT MORE

BOOKS

Dickinson, Rachel. *Tools of the Ancient Romans: A Kid's Guide to the History & Science of Life in Ancient Rome*. Norwich, VA: Nomad Press, 2006.

Lassieur, Allison. *The Ancient Romans*. New York: Franklin Watts, 2004.

Nardo, Don. *From Founding to Fall: A History of Rome*. San Diego: Lucent Books, 2003.

Nardo, Don. *Julius Caesar: Roman General and Statesman*. Minneapolis: Compass Point Books, 2009.

Visit this Scholastic Web site for more information on Ancient Rome:
www.factsfornow.scholastic.com
Enter the keywords **Ancient Rome**

INDEX

Page numbers in *italics* indicate a photograph or map.

ABOUT THE AUTHOR

Peter Benoit is a graduate of Skidmore College in Saratoga Springs, New York. A lifelong learner and voracious reader, he balances his time between writing and tutoring students at all levels in mathematics and the sciences. He has written dozens of books for Children's Press on topics as diverse as ecosystems, Native American tribes, American history, and disasters. His interest in the classical world began early with reading the Greek and Roman myths as a primary school student. He began to study the history and literature of the classical period intensively in high school, and developed a gift for reading and translating Latin. He used this to read from primary sources and deepen his understanding of the ancient world at the collegiate level. Peter lives in Greenwich, New York.